The Boyhood of Pope John XXIII

A story about Angelo Joseph Roncalli

written by Anne McGravie
illustrated by Kathryn Shoemaker

ISBN: 0-03-049446-X
Library of Congress Catalog Card Number: 78-65519

Winston Press 430 Oak Grove Minneapolis, MN 55403

Almost one hundred years ago in Italy a baby boy was born who would grow up to be very important and change many people's lives. His name was Angelo Joseph Roncalli.

Angelo was born on a cold, dark November morning. Wind and rain from the mountains swept through the village streets. The villagers stayed home, huddled over their fires.

Upstairs in the Roncalli house, Marianna

Roncalli lay in bed with her new-born son. Covers were heaped over them, to keep out the cold.

Marianna's husband, John, and their two little girls smiled down at the baby.

"You're a big, strong boy," the father said. "Someday, you'll help me farm."

Then John Roncalli told his wife, "We must take the baby to church right away, so that he can be baptized."

That afternoon, John and Marianna trudged through the narrow village streets to the church. The cold wind blew in their faces, but the new baby in John's arms was warmly wrapped in a big shawl.

When they got to the church, the door was closed and locked.

"Where can Father Rebuzzini be?" John asked, hugging their baby closer.

"Perhaps he's gone to the city," said Marianna. "Let's go home and come back in the morning."

John shook his head. "I won't bring the baby home until he is baptized," he said.

Marianna thought of their other children. "I'll go home to take care of the girls," she said. "You stay, but keep the baby warm." Then she kissed Angelo and hurried home.

John stood in the cold and windy doorway of the church, waiting for the priest. The baby slept in his arms.

At last, Father Rebuzzini arrived. "What are you doing here so late?" he asked.

"I want you to baptize our son, Father," John Roncalli said proudly. "His name is to be Angelo Joseph."

The priest quickly unlocked the door.

"Come in," he said. "Bring your baby in out of the cold! Do you want him to get sick?"

But the baby was warm and happy. He didn't begin to cry until the priest gently poured water over his head to baptize him.

"Listen to him yell," said John Roncalli proudly. "My Angelino is a strong baby." (Angelino is a nickname for Angelo. It means "little angel.")

When John Roncalli got home that night, the whole village was there to welcome him and Baby Angelino. They drank to the child's good health with wine made from John Roncalli's own grapes.

"He's a fine child," one neighbor said. "You will be proud of him someday."

Another neighbor said, "It's been a long time since one of our village boys became a

priest. Perhaps Angelino will grow up to be a priest and serve God."

"Who knows?" an old woman said. "He may even be pope!" (The pope is the head of the Catholic Church.)

Then everyone laughed. But John Roncalli said, "Angelo is going to be a farmer and help me work the land."

The Roncallis rented a small piece of land but they dreamed of owning their own vineyard someday. (A vineyard is a field of grape vines.)

John Roncalli needed sons to help him work in the vineyard, and he thought that Angelo would love farming as much as he did.

But Baby Angelino cried whenever he was taken to the fields. And when he was old enough to walk, he ran off home when he thought no one was looking.

His father had to admit that Angelo did not seem to like farming.

"But he's very young," his father thought. "Maybe when he's a little older. . ."

Soon Angelino had two little brothers. His home was always full of children, because the Roncallis lived with their cousins. All together, the two families had ten children.

Angelino was a happy child, and very roly-poly, too. The Roncallis were poor, but they always had enough to eat. And they had many good times.

Sometimes, on a holiday, Angelino's Uncle Barba would pile all the children into a donkey cart and take them on a picnic.

On the way, they would stop at a shrine. (A shrine is a place with a statue or picture of a holy person.)

"Everybody out, we're going to pray," Uncle Barba would shout. And he would lead the prayers. Uncle Barba loved God very much, and he also loved to read. After the grown-ups finished their work for the day, Uncle Barba always sat down with the Bible or a Church newspaper. Angelino would crawl into his lap and listen to him read aloud.

When Angelino was five, he went to the little village school. "What are you going to be when you grow up, Angelo?" his teacher asked.

Angelo frowned as he thought about this question. "Well, I don't want to be a farmer," he said.

The teacher smiled. "Work hard and learn as much as you can. Someday you will know what you want to do with your life," he said.

Angelino liked school and learned very quickly. The teacher told Father Rebuzzini about him.

"Perhaps Angelo will be a priest when he grows up," the priest said. "But he will have to go to a bigger school to learn what he will need to know."

Father Rebuzzini sent Angelino to a school five miles away. He walked to and from school every day, carrying his shoes to keep them from getting worn out. Every morning, his mother gave him a slice of cold polenta for lunch. (Polenta is a cooked cereal made from cornmeal. When it is cold, it is thick enough to cut into pieces.)

Angelino studied arithmetic and geography, and he even began to learn Latin. (Latin is a language. Many important prayers of the Catholic Church were written in Latin.)

In the evening, Father Rebuzzini helped Angelo with his Latin. "I like these special lessons even more than going to school," Angelino told a friend. "I always get a cake or a piece of candy when I do well."

By the time Angelo was ten years old, he had learned a great deal. He told his younger brothers about his studies as they worked in the fields. And sometimes Angelo talked about leaving their village.

"Why can't Angelino be like our other sons?" John would ask Marianna. "They like farming!"

"Angelino is different," Marianna would reply.

Every night, the Roncallis prayed together. And every morning, Angelino went to church with his family. There he heard about the life and teachings of Jesus. Besides that, he learned more about Jesus in his lessons.

Angelino thought about how Jesus asked his friends to love and help one another. And day after day, Angelino saw how hard his father worked for the family he loved.

"What can I do to help other people and serve God?" Angelino wondered. "Could I ever be a priest?"

One day, Angelo ran home from his lesson to find his father.

"Papa," Angelo began excitedly, "Father Rebuzzini says I'm ready to go to school in the city. It won't cost you any money."

"I'm sorry, Angelino, but you can't go," said his father. "I have just bought a house and a small vineyard. Now I need you to help more than ever. Who knows? Even yet, you may become a good farmer!"

Angelo didn't know what to say. He felt that he just *had* to go to school, but he hated to disappoint his father. So Angelo went to see Father Rebuzzini.

"What can I do?" Angelo asked the priest.

Angelo was too shy to say that he might become a priest someday. But Father Rebuzzini knew what he was thinking.

"I will speak with your father," the priest said.

A few weeks later, it was moving day for the Roncalli family. The villagers came to the new home to celebrate, bringing gifts of food.

The Roncallis and their friends were having a happy party together when the door opened and Father Rebuzzini came in. Angelino went to him at once, and the priest put an arm around the boy's shoulders. Together they went to John Roncalli.

"What do you want your son to be?" the priest asked John Roncalli. "A good priest, or a bad farmer?"

Angelo held his breath as his father looked at him.

"If I let you go, will you study hard?" John Roncalli asked his son.

"Very hard, Papa," Angelo answered.

Then he began to laugh for joy, and all his friends and neighbors and family began to laugh too. Just think! Angelino, a boy from their own village, was going away to school and maybe someday he would be a priest!

After many years of study in the city, Angelo became a priest. And many, many years later, he became the pope, just as his neighbor had said. As pope, Angelo took the name John, his father's name. He became Pope John XXIII.

Pope John helped people understand each other and be friends. Some people called him the loving pope, because he loved children and old people, good people and bad people, rich people and poor people, people from everywhere in the world.

"We are all God's children," he said. "We are brothers and sisters, and we must love one another always."

And people everywhere loved Pope John because he was kind and humble and wise. Many people said that John XXIII, the farm boy who became pope, was one of the best popes the Catholic Church ever had.

A Biographical Sketch of Pope John XXIII

Angelo Giuseppi Roncalli was born November 25, 1881, in the village of Sotto il Monto ("Under the Mountain") in Bergamo, in the north of Italy.

Guided and tutored by the local parish priest, Don Francesco Rebuzzini, young Roncalli was able to continue his education and become a priest, instead of the farmer his father expected him to be.

Ordained in 1904, Father Roncalli took part in the Italian labor movement, and was drafted into the Italian army where he served first as a soldier, then as a chaplain in World War I. Later he opened associations for university students, and then began a career as Vatican emissary, representing the pope in Turkey, Bulgaria, Greece, and France. He soon established a reputation as a friendly, human, accessible person. In 1953, he became a Cardinal and the Patriarch of Venice.

Most people thought that John's election as pope in 1958 at the age of seventy-seven was intended to provide an interim papacy. But to the astonishment of the church and the world, he called an ecumenical (general) council, the Second Vatican Council, which met in 1962. At this meeting, the bishops of the Catholic Church reconsidered what images were best suited to the Catholic Church in today's world and went back to the biblical way of understanding the church. The old simplicity of the liturgy was restored, and the Council wrote documents considering the dignity of the human person, religious freedom, social justice, revelation, ecumenism, and the participation of lay people in the church.

John's fame, assured by his calling of the Council and by his work for world peace, was immeasurably enhanced by his winning personality — a combination of frank good humor and warm kindness. He was often called good Pope John, and at his death in 1963 he was universally mourned.